ALL IN ORPHAN CARE

SMALL GROUP CURRICULUM

Copyright © 2014 by Arrow Foundation
Written by Jason Johnson
Foreword by Mark Tennant

Published by Arrow Publishing

ISBN-13: 978-0-69222-672-8
ISBN-10: 0-692-22672-9

For more information, please visit
ALLINORPHANCARE.COM

ALL IN
ORPHAN CARE

SMALL GROUP CURRICULUM

JASON JOHNSON

WITH ARROW FOUNDATION

ALL IN
ORPHAN CARE

WESTMINSTER CONFESSION

In adoption, believers are taken into the number of God's children and enjoy the liberties and privileges of that relationship; they are given his name; they receive the Spirit of adoption; they have access to the throne of grace with boldness; and they are enabled to cry, "Abba, Father." Like a father, God has compassion on, protects, provides for, and chastens them; yet, they will never be cast off, but are sealed to the day of redemption, and will inherit the promises as heirs of everlasting salvation.

— Wesminster Confession of Faith, Chapter 12

TABLE
OF
CONTENTS
–

A Story of Redemption
Foreword by Mark Tennant

How To Use This Study

Why The Church Must Care For Orphans
Introduction by Jason Johnson

Head, Heart & Hands Paradigm

Spiritual Gifts Survey

About Arrow

    Arrow Child & Family Ministries

    Arrow Foundation

    Mark Tennant, Founder

About The Author

A STORY OF REDEMPTION

—

Mark Tennant, Founder/President, Arrow Foundation

In 1972, there were 320,000 children in foster care — of which I was one. At the age of 11 years old, a story full of tragedy, darkness and feelings of being trapped with no way of escape began to unfold in my life. I fell prey to an alcoholic and violent man in my home, which led to me enduring emotional, physical and sexual abuse. My only outlet was to hope, pray and wait for love and security to come from a seemingly powerless mom. In the end, she would run for the rescue of the abuser rather than toward me — the abused.

I was left alone to tend to the needs of my younger sister; and I would become her protector and defender until the day, when through court intervention, I was removed from my home and separated from her and everything else I had ever known. I left with nothing. One morning I got on the bus and left for school having no idea that by that evening I would be placed in foster care – never having said goodbye. I would never return to live with my family under the same roof.

For the next couple of years, I was moved from home to home in foster care with no real certainty about the future, until the day the people I now call mom and dad stepped into my life. For the next 5 years, before turning 18, Bill and Joan Mack, and all of their extended family poured themselves into my life. They gave of themselves to me and introduced me to a God who would give me a future and a hope — always reassuring me that I would be their son and I would have a family and a home with them forever, no matter what. While I may have left their home at 18, I did not leave their family. Today they are my parents and the grandparents to my kids. They are mine and I am theirs. Forever.

In 1972, I was one of those kids; but in 1992, I founded Arrow Child & Family Ministries to help those kids who were just like me.

Over the past 23 years, Arrow has served approximately 40,000 children in foster care and within the past seven years, helped 2,000 children find their forever family through adoption. This is what we do — offer hope and healing by bringing families to children. God has done this for us through Jesus. We are therefore compelled to do the same for them.

The Church has always been at the core of who we are at Arrow and is central to our mission of helping kids and strengthening families. In 2007, we started transforming our mindset from being agency driven to becoming ministry driven. I began to challenge Arrow leadership and staff to consider the expansion of our role to also resource and equip the local church to serve alongside us and to rise up in their own way to impact child welfare in their community. The focus of this initiative would not solely be about churches supporting Arrow in its mission, but about Arrow finding ways to support local churches as they participated in the mission of God. This transformation goes beyond the occasional drop-off of flyers, bulletin inserts, posters and other propaganda to the church in a "drive-by relationship." Instead, Arrow is focused on forming a commitment to intentional relationships within churches. We recognize that only one entity has the capacity, the diversity and the mandate to care of the orphans of our society — that is the Church.

In 1972, I was one of those kids; but in 1992, I founded Arrow Child & Family Ministries to help those kids who were like I once was.

Most agencies focus on recruiting rather than operating as catalysts to inspire the development of church-based "orphan care" ministries that will serve and support the entirety of those called to engage in some capacity. In fact, most agencies within child welfare have seen the heartbreaking disruptions that occur when a family does not have adequate support. On the other hand, with a church-based orphan care ministry, support systems are provided by the church within the church setting. This resource, in turn, allows everyone to go ALL IN to meet the needs of children and families, and everyone has a place to serve.

In moving away from the drive-by mentality, we had to figure out what intentional relationships would look like to equip and resource churches. This shift was critical for Arrow. For the first time, the discussion was about true partnerships with give-and-take from both sides and not just "taking" on our side. We recognized that we have the ability to strengthen the local church through training in child abuse issues as well as educate them on what to look for and how to report abuse in an appropriate and timely manner. Also, the Arrow staff has the knowledge and skills needed to discuss a family's options in exploring the foster care and adoption processes. We are also able to educate the church by providing a clear picture of the community it serves through a current snapshot of child welfare and families in crisis, as well as inform them about the unique needs of their community and impactful ways to respond.

In the fall of 2013, Arrow Child & Family Ministries formed Arrow Foundation, an affiliate organization committed to equipping the Church to help kids and strengthen families. The mission of Arrow Foundation is, in part, to engage and equip the Church to care for the marginalized, the oppressed, the neglected, the abused and the orphaned through foster care, adoption, family support services and other alternative forms of care. The objective is simple: We want to help kids and strengthen families by providing resources to facilitate that culture within the Church.

We recognize that great efforts have gone forth to educate the Church about the orphan care issue, but we believe there is significantly more to do for the Church to be fully prepared to participate in this calling. To address this, Jason Johnson has masterfully compiled a study that is theologically sound and relevant for all those considering their place of service in orphan care ministry. Through the ALL IN Orphan Care resources, you will be challenged, encouraged, compelled and inspired to go ALL IN to care for the least of these.

As I was able to experience redemption in my own life, I want nothing less for those who are marginalized, oppressed and orphaned in the years to come. It's on us, the redeemed and adopted ones of God, to extend the grace we have received through Jesus into the lives of those who are like I once was. It's time for the Church to go ALL IN. This book will help guide you to discern your response to that call.

I want to personally say, thank you. Thank you for standing in the gap for kids like me. I am confident that I would not be where I am today had someone like you not intervened on my behalf. You are making an eternal impact in the lives of children and families far more than you could possibly imagine. Thank you for being willing to be used by God in the lives of these kids so that a world that is orphaned from Him might have a profound taste of what redemption, restoration, hope and healing can look like.

God is still writing stories on the pages of kids' hearts. Bill and Joan Mack chose to become a part of mine. Will you choose to become a part of one of the many in need?

My thoughts and prayers are with you as you consider this calling,

Mark Tennant

HOW TO USE THIS STUDY

—

NO LEADER NECESSARY

Our hope is that this workbook is as accessible and user friendly as possible so that any group could pick it up and use it, whether there is a designated "leader" or not. The material is written so that members of the group can share responsibilities to read and help navigate everyone else through different sections.

Each session begins with a short 2-minute "launch" video that helps cast vision for the session and launch the group into their study. You can find these videos at **allinorphancare.com/launch**.

SESSION OUTLINES

Each session is organized around five primary sections: PRAY, CONNECT, GROW, DISCUSS and REFLECT.

Here's a brief description of each:

PRAY — Begin each group meeting with prayer. Give each group member the opportunity to share any particular requests they would like the group to pray for. This is an important time to encourage one another and focus your hearts and minds on what God may have in store during your meeting.

CONNECT — Take this opportunity to catch up on what's going on in each other's lives. How has your week been? Did anything out of the ordinary or particularly interesting happen? Use the "Share Your Story" component of this section to help gear the group's thoughts around the theme of the study.

GROW — This is the study portion. Each session includes scripture passages, commentary and discussion questions to read. As you work through this section, either a) assign one person to facilitate the whole section or b) ask different group members to facilitate different parts.

DISCUSS — As you close each group meeting spend 5-10 minutes discussing main ideas and application points from the study. What stood out to you the most? Why? This section is intended to provide the group the opportunity to process and think aloud together before leaving.

REFLECT — Each group member is encouraged to personally process and apply some of the things they are learning. This reflection resource can also be something to look back on one day so participants can see all God has done since they began working through this material. Some space to write is provided in this workbook, or you can use your own journal if more space is required.

HEAD, HEART & HANDS PARADIGM

A unique feature of this study is what we call the "Fully-Integrated Paradigm: Head, Heart and Hands." This approach to the study seeks to balance the attention we are paying to what we must learn (head), what we must feel (heart) and what we must do (hands).

Before beginning the first session, have the group read the "Head, Heart and Hands" Paradigm material found on page 24.

STORIES

As an added resource to your study, visit **allinorphancare.com/stories** to watch inspiring stories from people who are following God's call to help kids and strengthen families. These short videos can be viewed in your group setting to help reinforce an idea being studied or to simply inspire and challenge the group through the experiences of others.

WHY THE CHURCH MUST CARE FOR ORPHANS

—

Jason Johnson, Director of Church Engagement, Arrow Foundation

It was never God's intent for children to be without a family. Among the unending evidences that we live in a fatally sin-scarred world, this specific consequence particularly pains the heart of God. This is why Scripture says He *"executes justice for the fatherless"* (Deuteronomy 10:18) and assumes the role of *"the father of the fatherless"* (Psalm 68:5). This is the heart of God, a good, loving and gracious Father.

If you were to read the Bible from the very beginning to the very end, several themes would surface that are consistent throughout the narrative of Scripture. Things like God's power, God's mercy and God's faithfulness, or man's weakness, rebellion and ultimate need for redemption. These and many others fill the pages of both the Old and New Testaments, telling a beautiful story of God's relentless pursuit of His people whom He loves.

Yet, of all the themes to be found within the pages of Scripture, one that shines with unparalleled clarity and stands with an unmatched prominence and stature is: *God secures and protects the rights of the helpless and the hopeless*. From the beginning of time to the very end, God intercedes on behalf of the needy and offers to them the abundance of His sufficiency. That which particularly pains His heart unequivocally drives his actions. He sets His pursuit on filling the empty, embracing the marginalized and healing the broken and destitute in Jesus. The Apostle Paul in 2 Corinthians 8:9 articulates it this way:

> " ... *you know the grace of our Lord Jesus Christ, that though he was rich, yet for your sake he became poor, so that you by his poverty might become rich.*"

This is the gospel, that while we were empty and impoverished in our sin, the riches of the grace of God in Jesus freely and fully filled us. We simply cannot escape this theme in Scripture, but it doesn't end there ...

The Bible expects that what particularly pains God's heart would particularly pain ours, and what unequivocally drives His actions would undoubtedly drive ours. The benefits of God's abundance poured into us when we were empty and destitute do not terminate on us. Rather, they are to be extended into the lives of others who are marginalized and oppressed and orphaned. So now, following the pattern of how God consistently works, we are called to *"give justice to the weak and fatherless"* (Psalm 82:3) and to *"seek justice, correct oppression [and] bring justice to the fatherless"* (Isaiah 1:16-17). As seekers of justice and correctors of oppression, **we care for abused, neglected and orphaned children because we have been cared for in Jesus**; we seek justice for them because justice has been won for us in Jesus; we rescue them from their plights because we, in Jesus, have been rescued from ours; we adopt the orphan, because as the Apostle Paul writes, Jesus came *"so that we might receive adoption"* (Galatians 4:5). His work on our behalf becomes the motivation behind our work on theirs.

. . . .

We care for abused, neglected and orphaned children because we have been cared for in Jesus.

. . . .

This leads us to the clarion call in the New Testament, admonishing us to care for orphans, and provides some context as to why we should. In the Christian life, we can demonstrate our faith in God in a variety of ways – i.e. prayer, giving, worship, serving, etc. The means by which our faith can express itself are seemingly endless and full of possibilities. Yet, in James 1:27, we are told that of all the measures by which our faith can be demonstrated, caring for orphans in their distress ranks among the highest and purest.

> *"Religion that is pure and undefiled before God, the Father, is this: to visit orphans and widows in their affliction, and to keep oneself unstained from the world."*

Why would God hold the care of orphans in such high regard? Why does He rank it among the highest expressions of our faith? Perhaps because **caring for the marginalized, oppressed and orphaned is not only one of the clearest expressions of the heart of God but also one of the most tangible demonstrations of the gospel this world will ever see.** If the gospel is ultimately the story of those who were empty in sin and orphaned from God, being adopted into His family by the work of Jesus, then our care for and adoption of vulnerable, neglected, abused, marginalized and orphaned children is a beautiful continuation of the redemption story of God and a vivid demonstration of the love of Jesus extended through us. Again, our care of orphans is rooted in God's care of us through Jesus – it begins not with the orphan "out there" who needs a family but with the orphan in us that has been given one in Jesus.

. . . .

Caring for the marginalized, oppressed and orphaned is not only one of the clearest expressions of the heart of God but also one of the most tangible demonstrations of the gospel this world will ever see.

. . . .

This is the foundation our study is built upon – God's heart for the marginalized, the theology of our adoption and our gospel-centered response to the need around us. It is our great hope that as the gospel of our adoption in Jesus is pressed into our hearts more deeply, our desire to demonstrate that redemption story to others would grow more widely. Our encouragement to you is to discern how the Holy Spirit may lead you in light of the truths you will discover together through this study, and that in doing so you may be stretched to dream bigger dreams and believe greater things for how, and when and where God may want to use you to seek justice, correct oppression and care for the marginalized, abused and orphaned.

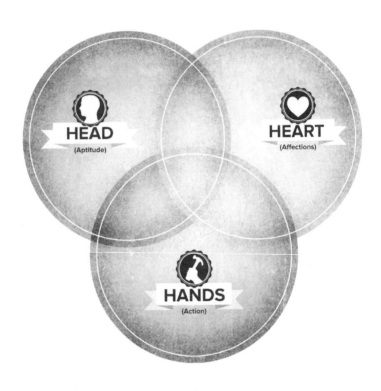

THE HEAD, HEART & HANDS PARADIGM

—

As Christians, we are called to love and serve God with every aspect of our being. In Mark 12:30, Jesus quotes an Old Testament commandment when He says, *"You shall love the Lord your God with all your heart and with all your soul and with all your mind and with all your strength."* Scripture is not compartmentalizing the ways in which we love and serve God, as if we can turn the soul off and move into the mind category, or momentarily set aside the strength compartment while we operate out of the heart. Rather, the Old Testament command quoted in the New Testament by Jesus is a timeless, holistic one, meant to illustrate that no part of who we are is exempt from being used to know and love God, and all parts are used together as one in serving Him.

To simplify the idea, think of the Christian faith as being rooted in our knowing, loving and serving God with our HEAD (mind), our HEART (soul) and our HANDS (strength).

These three dimensions — head, heart and hands — are not mutually exclusive or isolated from one another. Rather, each feeds and sustains the others by helping to form a unified and "fully integrated" self.

When taken in isolation, our faith becomes fragmented, over-accentuating one dimension to the neglect of the others. For example, if our faith is primarily HEAD-based, we may rely heavily on knowledge of God without ever having a truly close or intimate relationship with Him. Or, if our faith is primarily HANDS-based we may do a lot for God but not ever form a strong grasp on what we believe about Him as Scripture teaches. Or, if our faith is primarily HEART-based we may experience very emotional, mystical moments with God that are not rooted in an understanding of the truth of who He is or are detached from a biblically grounded relationship with Him.

Jesus exposes the fragmented faith of people on several occasions in Scripture, with one of the most notable being found in Matthew 7:21-23:

> *"Not everyone who says to me, 'Lord, Lord,' will enter the kingdom of heaven, but the one who does the will of my Father who is in heaven. On that day many will say to me, 'Lord, Lord, did we not prophesy in your name, and cast out demons in your name, and do many mighty works in your name?' And then will I declare to them, 'I never knew you; depart from me...'*

In other words, many will rely on the works of their HANDS only to find that their HEARTS were never close to Him. Some will give their time and energy to the things of God but will never actually give their lives to Him. This is a fragmented faith that in the end leads to missing out on what God has in store for us.

We could go on. The point, however, is that by themselves none of these dimensions can do justice to the fullness of the capacity God has given us to know and love and serve Him with our whole selves. Our faith must not be fragmented, but rather a fully integrated make-up of the whole of who we are otherwise our aptitude (head), affections (heart) and actions (hands) can never be truly utilized to the capacity God intended.

FULLY-INTEGRATED ORPHAN CARE

Why spend so much time on knowing, loving and serving God in a fully integrated way? Because this will act as the framework through which we respond to His mandate to care for the marginalized, oppressed and orphaned around us. At the end of the day it's not enough to know God's heart on the matter (head) and never do anything about it (hands), or to feel strongly about the issues of justice (heart) with no real grasp on the biblical call to care for orphans (head) and no real actions that are doing anything about it (hands). It's one thing to care about orphans; it's an entirely different thing to care for them. One is head or heart centered; the other drives the actions of our hands. This is the intent of our study — to identify how each of us are called not just to care *about*, but to care *for* the marginalized, abused, neglected and orphaned.

Even now as we begin this study, some hold to right beliefs about orphan care but their actions are not following suit. Some are very emotionally invested but do not have a firm grasp on what God has to say on the matter. Others are sincerely concerned about the issues and are involved in matters of justice but are being driven by their own efforts or recognition, not the heart of God. Wherever you may be now, the intent of this study is to lead us all into a further developing and maturing understanding of what it means for us as individuals, groups, churches and communities to be fully-integrated in our faith and lives.

At the end of the day, if we pursue the care of the abused, neglected and orphaned in a fragmented way, our right thoughts will only get us so far, our strong emotions will last but a while, and our good works will eventually become exhausting efforts. The only sustainable way for us to respond by faith to what God is calling us to do is to be fully integrated in our approach, with right beliefs, right emotions and right actions working in harmony with one another. Then, when one part is weak (say for instance the work is especially grueling and we are tempted to quit), the others will help guide and sustain (our beliefs that the work is pleasing to God and worth it will motivate us to keep going).

Throughout this study, you will be asked to use the HEAD-HEART-HANDS paradigm to apply the truths we are learning and discussing in each session — i.e. What biblical truth do we learn from this? How does what we are discussing move you and make you feel? What are you going to do in response to what we have learned together? This is a critical component of this study and will act as a starting point for what will prove to be some very encouraging and helpful dialogue.

WHAT IS ORPHAN CARE?

—

What pains the heart of God must pain ours, and what drives the hands of God must drive ours.

Before you begin, watch the Launch Video: Session 1
at www.allinorphancare.com/launch to help get you started.

PRAY

—

As you gather the group together, begin with prayer. Each group member should have the opportunity to share any particular requests they would like the group to pray for. Use this time as an opportunity to encourage one another and focus your hearts and minds on what God may have in store during your time together.

CONNECT

—

If any group members do not already know each other, introduce yourselves and share a little of your story. Answer questions like:

- ◆ Where were you born?
- ◆ What brought you to this city?
- ◆ Are you married? (If so, for how long? How did you meet?)
- ◆ Do you have kids? (If so, how many?)
- ◆ What do you do for a living?
- ◆ Etc.

Spend the next 5-10 minutes connecting as a group. Catch up on what's going on in each other's lives.

- ◆ How has your week been?
- ◆ Did anything out of the ordinary or particularly interesting happen?

♦ Is anything coming up for you between now and the next group meeting that you want group members to know?

Why Are You Here?

During this first session, it is important to discuss why everyone has chosen to attend this group and go through a study on caring for orphans. As much as you are able, share:

> Where are you in the process of caring for orphans?
> Why did you feel particularly led by God to go through this study?
> What do you hope to gain from going through this study and being part of this group?

GROW

—

Before You Begin: Read the "Why The Church Must Care For Orphans" found on page 19 together as a group. Either a) have different members read portions out loud or, b) give each member a few minutes to read silently on their own.

~ New

(Why Are We Called To "Orphan Care"?)

As we saw in the study introduction, the care of orphans is a response to the heart of God to bring justice to the marginalized and families to the fatherless. It is allowing what drives His actions towards the lowly and destitute to drive ours in similar fashion. The theme of God protecting the helpless and hopeless is paramount throughout Scripture, and the mandate to spend our lives doing the same is unavoidable.

God's Heart for Justice

READ:
Deuteronomy 10:18 —

> *He executes justice for the fatherless and the widow, and*
> *loves the sojourner, giving him food and clothing.*

Psalm 68:5 —

> *Father of the fatherless and protector of widows is God in*
> *His holy habitation.*

* What do these passages teach us about God's heart for
  justice?
* What do we learn about His actions towards the
  marginalized and destitute?

Of all the evidences that this world is not as it should be, none seem
to be more paramount to the heart of God than when injustices rule,
oppression runs rampant and children are left to fend for themselves
without the loving and nurturing support of a family.

. . . .

**Transformation of status for the lowly, the humanly
hopeless, as they experience the hand of God
reaching into their situation, is possibly the most
pervasive theme of biblical writings.
– Dallas Willard**

. . . .

Our Call To Reflect God's Heart

READ:
Psalm 82:3 —

> *Give justice to the weak and the fatherless; maintain the*
> *right of the afflicted and the destitute.*

Isaiah 1:17 —

> *... seek justice, correct oppression; bring justice to the*
> *fatherless; plead the widow's cause.*

- What do these passages reveal about God's expectations of us?

- How does our seeking of justice and correcting of oppression put God's heart for these things on display in this world?

Our identity is defined by the heart of God – we are seekers of justice and correctors of oppression. Our activity is fueled by the hand of God – we are to care for the very things His hand is uniquely extended towards. In other words, we are an extension of the heart of God by living as the hand of God in this world.

Our Unique Call to Care For Orphans

READ:
James 1:27

> Religion that is pure and undefiled before God, the Father, is this: to visit orphans and widows in their affliction, and to keep oneself unstained from the world.

- Why does God hold up the care of orphans as a "pure and undefiled" expression of our faith?

When Does a Child Become an "Orphan"?

The mandate is clear – we are to reflect the heart of God in our care of orphans. However, in recent times the term "orphan" has taken on a shape and life of its own, used in a variety of contexts to refer to a variety of situations in which children are in need of care. For the purposes of our study, we want to establish a clear understanding of what we mean when we talk about "orphans" and our involvement in "orphan care:"

An "orphan" is:

- A child who has lost parents to death (Familial Orphan)

- A child whose birth parent(s) are functionally incapable of providing care because of abuse, neglect, addiction, endangerment, incarceration, etc. (Functional Orphan)

♦ A child whose birth parent(s) voluntarily or involuntarily relinquish their parental rights (Social Orphan)

In other words, an "orphan" is a child with no parental structure of safety, support, provision or care necessary in order to adequately manage the risk to which they are daily exposed. In this vulnerable position, they are in need of others to provide for them relationally what they have not been provided and are incapable of supplying on their own.

What Is "Orphan Care?"

So let's define what "orphan care" is. We will begin by first defining what it is *not* ...

"Orphan Care" is NOT:

1. Exclusively focused on international orphanages and adoptions

2. Establishing the institutional care of children as the end goal (i.e. orphanages, group homes)

3. Enabling or encouraging families to abandon their children

"Orphan Care" IS:

1. Seeking permanency placement for children (family reunification, kinship care or adoption)

2. Pursuing preventative measures to provide alternative care for families in order to prevent children from being removed from homes

3. Supporting those who are providing care for vulnerable children (through foster care, adoption or alternative measures of care)

DISCUSS

As you close your time together, spend 5-10 minutes processing the things you have learned and discussed. This is an especially important opportunity to share thoughts, feelings, questions, concerns or any resolutions you have made in response to your study.

- What truth or idea stood out to you most in this session? Why?

- Why is it important for us to understand the heart of God for the oppressed, marginalized and orphaned? How will this help sustain us in our call and support us when things get difficult?

- How has your understanding of "orphan care" been affirmed, changed or expanded during this session?

. . . .

Let my heart be broken by the things that break the heart of God. – Bob Pierce, Founder of World Vision

. . . .

REFLECT

As you reflect on the truths of this session and consider the personal implications for your own life, spend some time writing and processing through the following three questions:

- What are your hopes and expectations going into this process or continuing the process you have already begun?

- As of right now, what does "caring for orphans" look like for you and your family?

- Would you be willing to let God expand the parameters you have set? What fears, questions, anxieties or concerns do you have?

JOURNAL

—

_____

_____

_____

_____

_____

_____

_____

_____

_____

_____

_____

_____

_____

_____

_____

_____

_____

_____

_____

—

THE THEOLOGY OF OUR ADOPTION

—

Orphan care, like the Gospel, is a multi-generational story of redemption.

Before you begin, watch the Launch Video: Session 2
at www.allinorphancare.com/launch to help get you started.

PRAY

—

As you gather the group together, begin with prayer. Each group member should have the opportunity to share any particular requests they would like the group to pray for. Use this time as an opportunity to encourage one another and focus your hearts and minds on what God may have in store during your time together.

CONNECT

—

Spend the next 5-10 minutes connecting as a group. Catch up on what's going on in each other's lives.

- ◆ How has your week been?
- ◆ Did anything out of the ordinary or particularly interesting happen?
- ◆ Is anything coming up for you between now and the next group meeting that you want group members to know?

In Session 1, we learned about God's heart for justice and our responsibility to care for the marginalized and orphaned. In this session, we will explore how the gospel redeems our pasts, secures our present realities and shifts the trajectory of our futures forever. In light of that, we will discuss the implications as they pertain to our care of orphans.

To begin, have members of the group briefly share how Jesus has changed their pasts, presents and futures.

Examples:

- Jesus freed me from my past addiction, has given me a present reality of sobriety and protected me from a future that would have been plagued by the consequences of continuing in that broken pattern.

- My past was marked by broken relationships, but God has been gracious to give me a strong marriage and/or friendships today. I'm committed to commitment in these relationships forever.

- I experienced some horrendous things in my past, but God has graciously carried me through them all. I believe He wants to use my past hurts to help minister to others in the future.

GROW
—

A Multi-Generational Story

The imagery of adoption is used throughout Scripture to paint a vivid picture of the Gospel — God's rescuing and redeeming love for us in Jesus. Our salvation, or adoption into the family of God through Jesus, is presented as a multi-generational story of hope – breaking past cycles of brokenness, securing a new present reality and altering our future trajectory for all eternity. Because of the work of Christ on our behalf, we who were once isolated and orphaned in our sin have been adopted into the family of God as sons and daughters – and this changes everything forever!

. . . .

The deepest and strongest foundation of adoption is located not in the act of humans adopting humans, but in God adopting humans. And this act

is not part of His ordinary providence in the world; it is at the heart of the gospel. – John Piper

. . . .

The gospel of our adoption through Jesus into the family of God acts as the basis of our care for those who are family-less and in need of belonging. It is essential that we "get" the gospel deeply in our hearts so that we can effectively demonstrate the gospel widely in how we care for the oppressed, abused, marginalized and orphaned.

READ:
Galatians 4:4-7 —

> **4** *But when the fullness of time had come, God sent forth his Son, born of woman, born under the law,* **5** *to redeem those who were under the law, so that we might receive adoption as sons.* **6** *And because you are sons, God has sent the Spirit of his Son into our hearts, crying, "Abba! Father!"* **7** *So you are no longer a slave, but a son, and if a son, then an heir through God.*

Past Redeemed (v5)

What does this verse say was the two-fold purpose of God sending Jesus to this earth?

The phrase "were under the law" is in the past tense – What does this communicate about the effect the work of Jesus has had on our past sin, guilt, shame, isolation from God, etc.?

READ:
2 Corinthians 5:17 —

> *Therefore, if anyone is in Christ, he is a new creation. The old has passed away; behold, the new has come*

Psalm 103:12 —

> *... as far as the east is from the west, so far does he remove our transgressions from us.*

Romans 8:1 —

> *There is therefore now no condemnation for those who are in Christ Jesus.*

- ◆ How far has God's forgiveness reached into our past?
- ◆ Why do you think so many struggle with still feeling "condemned"?

Point: Through our faith in the life, death, burial and resurrection of Jesus, our past has been redeemed – we were once isolated and at odds with God in our sin ... but Jesus has reconciled, renewed and brought us near.

Present Secured (v6)

The term "Abba" is the Aramaic form of the word "Daddy" which denotes intimacy and affection. What does this verse teach us about where we stand with God positionally through the gospel? How does our present standing with Him contrast to where we once stood with Him in our sin (i.e. separated, condemned, etc.)?

. . . .

Adoption is the highest privilege that the gospel offers. – J.I. Packer

. . . .

READ
John 1:9-13 —

> *... to all who did receive him, who believed in his name, he gave the right to become children of God, who were born, not of blood nor of the will of the flesh nor of the will of man, but of God.*

James 1:17 —

> *Every good gift and every perfect gift is from above, coming down from the Father of lights with whom there is no variation or shadow due to change.*

Matthew 7:9-11

> *Which one of you, if his son asks him for bread, will give him a stone? Or if he asks for a fish, will give him a serpent? If you then, who are evil, know how to give good gifts to your children, how much more will your Father who is in heaven give good things to those who ask him!*

- ◆ What benefits and privileges do we presently live under as children of God?
- ◆ How have we come about receiving those?

Point: We live today with the full rights and privileges of being children of God. As our Father, He protects, provides, shows compassion and even disciplines us in love. We were once alienated, but now we are intimate. We do not come to Him with apprehension but with assurance, knowing we will always be accepted, listened to and loved by our "Abba."

Future Guranteed (v7)

An "heir" is someone who lives today with the guarantee of receiving something in the future. There is hope and assurance now in a promise that will be fully realized at some point in the future. What does this verse teach us about the future trajectory of our lives as sons and daughters of God?

READ:
1 Peter 1:3-5 —

> *Blessed be the God and Father of our Lord Jesus Christ! According to his great mercy, he has caused us to be born again to a living hope through the resurrection of Jesus Christ from the dead, to an inheritance that is imperishable, undefiled, and unfading, kept in heaven for you, who by God's power are being guarded through faith for a salvation ready to be revealed in the last time.*

Ephesians 1:13-14 —

In him you also, when you heard the word of truth, the gospel of your salvation, and believed in him, were sealed with the promised Holy Spirit, who is the guarantee of our inheritance until we acquire possession of it, to the praise of his glory.

Romans 8:15-17 —

For you did not receive the spirit of slavery to fall back into fear, but you have received the Spirit of adoption as sons, by whom we cry, "Abba! Father!" The Spirit himself bears witness with our spirit that we are children of God, and if children, then heirs—heirs of God and fellow heirs with Christ...

- ◆ How should hope, assurance and confidence in the future change the way we live today?
- ◆ What are some practical examples you can give?

Point: Our future in Christ is promised to be full of glory. It may not be without its difficulty along the way, but we can trust that no matter what happens around us, there is an inheritance waiting for us that cannot be taken away from us. The future trajectories of our lives have been eternally changed.

The gospel is a multi-generational story of redemption. It breaks our past cycles, forms our new realities and offers us a future hope unburdened by the broken contexts from which we originated. God changes our names. He gives us new identities. He grants us the rights and privileges of being His sons and daughters. He secures our futures and changes the trajectory of our lives forever.

Why Talk About The Gospel So Much?

You may be asking this question – *I thought this study was about orphan care, so why are we spending so much time talking about the gospel?* That's a great question! The answer is simple: Orphan care does not begin with the child "out there" who needs a family but with the child in us who's been given one in Jesus. The gospel in us is where we begin, but it does not terminate there. The end goal is for the story of the gospel in us to be declared and demonstrated through us into the lives of those around us — and in the interests of our particular study, into the lives of marginalized, abused, neglected and orphaned kids.

As the gospel story of redemption is being told in our lives, we have the opportunity to see the same story brought to bear in theirs. Orphan care, like the gospel, is a multi-generational story of hope and love — it works to break past cycles of brokenness, form new realities of love and change the future trajectories of kids' lives in ways that otherwise would not have been available to them.

Questions to Consider:

- Where do you think you would be right now had Jesus not interceded in your life when He did?

- How can you intercede in the life of a child so that one day they may say, "I can't imagine where I would be right now had _____ not stepped into my life?"

DISCUSS
As you close your time together, spend 5-10 minutes processing the things you have learned and discussed. This is an especially important opportunity to share thoughts, feelings, questions, concerns or any resolutions you have made in response to your study.

1. What truth or idea stood out to you most in this session? Why?

2. In your own words, describe how the gospel and our care of orphans are both "multi-generational" stories.

3. Why is it so important for us to understand the theology of the gospel as it pertains to our care of orphans?

REFLECT

As you reflect on the truths of this session and consider the personal implications for your own life, spend some time writing and processing through the following three questions:

1. Looking back on your life, how do you see the faithfulness of God working through your past to bring you to the point where you are today?

2. If you could measure your current posture of worship towards Jesus and celebration in the gospel on a scale of 1-10, with 1 being near apathetic and 10 being pure adoration, where would you be right now? What are some specific things you can do to grow in your awareness of the gospel and affections for God?

3. In what ways do you need to actively take the "next steps" in demonstrating the gospel more widely to the marginalized, oppressed and orphaned around you?

JOURNAL

—

_____

_____

_____

_____

_____

_____

_____

_____

_____

_____

_____

_____

_____

_____

_____

_____

ADOPTION: FROM DARKNESS TO LIGHT

—

Kyle and Jennifer Sapaugh

Parents to five daugthers (so far!)
In-laws to one son-in-law (Dawn was married in
January, 2014.)

About eight years ago, I would have said, "Adoption: what a great option for those who can't conceive."

At that point, I had no idea of the path God had marked out for my family.

As close friends embarked on the adoption journey, this foreign idea of adoption began to surface in my mind. My heart began to change as I realized that while my three year old would wake up in our safe, secure world — watching her favorite cartoons while eating her favorite breakfast — there was a three year old just miles away waking up hungry, scared, neglected and alone.

The contrast was too great; it didn't seem right. My husband and I, so overwhelmed with the needs right around us, began discussing where God was leading our hearts. In June 2007, God showed us our next step. Five years into marriage, 24 years old, mother of a toddler and expecting baby #2, I received a phone call that forever changed our lives.

Dawn, a 17-year-old girl in my small group, who lived alone with her father just miles away, called me frantically. She had just found her dad dead. She was alone, scared, confused and lost. In that moment, in that phone call — all we knew was flipped upside down and our lives were changed forever.

Dawn was not the average 17-year-old American girl. In fact, Dawn wasn't American at all. She was Scottish. At the age of 13, after a tumultuous relationship with her mom, she was sent to live with her Dad (also Scottish) in the U.S. Only seeing him two times between the ages of six and 13, Dawn hardly knew him. Within a year after moving to America, her step-mom was tragically killed in a car accident. Dawn, now separated from her biological family, experiencing the loss of her step-mom, a second divorce from another step-mom and now the death of her dad, was in a place of rebellion, skirted in trauma and clothed in rejection. She was alone, rejected, hurt and lost. And that is how we got her.

Kyle and I vividly recount those first weeks. I rushed to get Dawn; Kyle came home from an out of town business trip. We began planning a funeral, dealing with Scottish relatives and immigration lawyers – meanwhile hosting Dawn and many of her unique friends.

It was chaos. It was heavy.

Dawn had nowhere to go. Biological family in Scotland wasn't an option and she was wanting to finish school in Texas, where she was — where we were.

We remember laying in bed — in silence. The air thick with the thoughts and fears and weight of what we knew we were about to do.

We knew we couldn't just "house" a teenager. We were trying to grow and protect our family and believed there would be too many unknowns with letting someone just stay with us. We had to have boundaries and house rules — she had to be a part of the family. We didn't know exactly what that meant, but we knew that's how it had to be. We began to pray that God would somehow weave it all together. Despite the losses, the awkwardness, the age gap (or lack there of), we prayed that God would make us a family. And so we adopted Dawn. As young parents in our mid-20's, we suddenly had a teenage daughter!

To say that this journey has been easy would be ridiculous. It has been hard, at times, very hard. We went from changing diapers, playing pretend and daydreaming of what baby #2 would look like, to cell phone rules, grade issues, dating, curfew, etc. — literally overnight. From spending every night after the kids went to bed alone together, to almost never spending time alone together. The weight of it all, at times, was hard on our marriage and on the little kids. We were in over our heads, for sure. But God was faithful.

We had no idea the challenges that would present themselves when we made our choice to envelop Dawn into our family. And as we reflect back, that was really perfect — because it was faith that we needed - oblivious to all the hard things that could come our way, only trusting in God's call on our lives. We are so blessed to have struggled and fought for Dawn these last 7 years. We are blessed to have seen her thrive and succeed, to grow and mature. It's a joy to now see our little girls' sweet adoration for their biggest sister. We love that they will never know anything different. Of all the beautiful things we have seen God do since Dawn became a part of our family, none is more amazing than seeing Dawn go from darkness to light and getting to watch her life today and her future path literally changed by the saving power of Jesus Christ.

For us, adoption has been one of the most amazing gifts God has ever given us. The privilege of getting to be a part of God's transforming power has been overwhelming. It has taught us that this life is indeed not about our comfort or our perfect plans. It is ultimately about His Kingdom, His power and His glory.

God uses adoption to change lives in a radical way.

We will never be the same, and we look forward to getting to adopt again in the future.

THE GOSPEL DISPLAYED IN ORPHAN CARE

—

The imagery of adoption is used throughout Scripture to paint a vivid picture of the Gospel – God's rescuing love for us through Jesus.

Before you begin, watch the Launch Video: Session 3 at www.allinorphancare.com/launch to help get you started.

PRAY

—

As you gather the group together, begin with prayer. Each group member should have the opportunity to share any particular requests they would like the group to pray for. Use this time as an opportunity to encourage one another and focus your hearts and minds on what God may have in store during your time together.

CONNECT

—

Spend the next 5-10 minutes connecting as a group. Catch up on what's going on in each other's lives.

- ◆ How has your week been?
- ◆ Did anything out of the ordinary or particularly interesting happen?
- ◆ Is anything coming up for you between now and the next group meeting that you want group members to know?

In Session 2, we learned about the multi-generational scope of the gospel in our lives – how it breaks pasts cycles, forms new present realities and alters the future trajectory of our lives forever. In this session, we will explore how the gospel of our adoption through Jesus is vividly and tangibly seen through our care of the marginalized, neglected, abused and orphaned of this world.

There's a variety of ways God allows us to "see" Him throughout our lives. To begin this session, share with the group different ways you "see" God in your daily life.

- ♦ What experiences, interactions and encounters do you find focus your mind and heart on Him the most?
- ♦ What draws your heart into worship of Him?
- ♦ What in your life right now is teaching you the most about the character and nature of who God is?

GROW
—

Three Ways The Gospel is Displayed Through Orphan Care

Let's explore three tangible ways we see the gospel demonstrated through our care of marginalized, oppressed, neglected and orphaned kids.

#1: Orphan care demands we interject ourselves into broken stories just as Jesus interjected Himself into ours.

READ:
Matthew 1:23 —

> *"Behold, the virgin shall conceive and bear a son, and they shall call his name Immanuel" (which means, God with us).*

Philippians 2:5-8 —

> *Have this mind among yourselves, which is yours in Christ Jesus, who, though he was in the form of God, did not count equality with God a thing to be grasped, but emptied himself, by taking the form of a servant, being born in the likeness of men. And being found in human form, he humbled himself by becoming obedient to the point of death, even death on a cross.*

This is what we celebrate at Christmas, right? That God saw the plight of humanity and, in response, humbled Himself by putting on flesh. He took the form of a servant and entered into our broken story in order to rescue and redeem us from it.

. . . .

The gospel of Jesus Christ means our families and churches ought to be at the forefront of the adoption of orphans close to home and around the world. – Russell Moore

. . . .

Jesus pulled us out of a broken story by first humbly and willingly being pulled into it. He joyfully accepted any and all implications that would come down on Him for our sake. In a similar way, as we engage in the care of the marginalized, abused, neglected and orphaned in this world, we must be willing to love them as Jesus has loved us by engaging them where they are, embracing the brokenness of where they come from and allowing their plight to change us, no matter the implications.

Orphan care is just as much about pulling a child out of a broken story as it is about you being pulled into one. In foster care, it could mean hard court hearings, navigating through an imperfect state-run child welfare system, difficult meetings with biological parents, case workers and lawyers and having your heart broken and world shattered by the difficult contexts which the child you are now caring for comes from. In adoption, it could mean engaging with a confused young lady going through an unexpected and unwanted pregnancy. It could mean persevering through the bureaucracy of overseas governments and officials overseeing institutional care in their country. It could mean developing long-term relationships with the biological family after adoption and navigating the often difficult relational roads that come along with that.

Caring for orphans is a beautiful thing, but it certainly is not a fairy tale. You will love more passionately, hurt more deeply, grieve more bitterly and celebrate more joyously throughout the process of caring for vulnerable children than you ever thought imaginable. This is the hard reality of where orphan care begins, where it takes you, what it requires of you and how it will break you. We must be willing to walk down this path for their sake. As we do, our loving embrace of their brokenness paints a vivid picture of how Jesus embraced ours.

#2: Orphan care requires that we stand for justice in a deeply spiritual battle just as Jesus, our true Hero, stood for us.

READ:
1 Timothy 2:5-6 —

> *For there is one God, and there is one mediator between God and men, the man Christ Jesus, who gave himself as a ransom for all, which is the testimony given at the proper time.*

1 John 2:1-2 —

> *My little children, I am writing these things to you so that you may not sin. But if anyone does sin, we have an advocate with the Father, Jesus Christ the righteous. He is the propitiation for our sins, and not for ours only but also for the sins of the whole world.*

The Bible describes Jesus as our "advocate" and "mediator," the One who testified before God on our behalf. He stood in the gap for us, destroying the rights of the enemy over our lives and assuming those rights upon Himself. He took full ownership of us and accepted the cost of His own life He would have to pay so that justice could be brought about in our lives.

In a similar way, our call is to fight for justice on behalf of the marginalized, oppressed and orphaned – to stand for them, advocate for them and assume responsibility for them. The gospel expects, albeit demands, that we be willing to stand for them where Jesus has stood for us, seeking justice in the midst of their brokenness.

However, in our fight for justice, we must be clear as to who the true enemy is that we are fighting against.

READ:
Ephesians 6:12 —

> *For we do not wrestle against flesh and blood, but against the rulers, against the authorities, against the cosmic powers over this present darkness, against the spiritual forces of evil in the heavenly places.*

John 10:10 —

> *The thief comes only to steal and kill and destroy. I came that they may have life and have it abundantly.*

The Bible says that in our fight for good over evil, we do not wrestle against any one person or group of people, but rather we fight against spiritual powers and authorities of darkness. In the end, the war we fight in orphan care is against a spiritual enemy who wants to steal, kill and destroy families.

In our standing for a child, we do not stand against their biological families, no matter the abuse, neglect or oppression they may be guilty of committing (especially in foster care situations). In many cases, it is heinous and our natural tendencies will be anger and bitterness towards them. However, in the end, as we stand for these kids, we do not necessarily stand against their parents but against the enemy who celebrates devastation and works towards injustice in their lives.

The real enemy in orphan care is not a biological mom or dad, but Satan who seeks to steal, kill and destroy families. It follows then since Satan is the real enemy, Jesus can be the only true hero. We must stand where He would stand on behalf of what He would stand for, not so we are seen as heroic but so He is seen as the ultimate hero in the battle for what is good and right and just. Any "hero complex" we have must be laid down so the true hero can be magnified.

#3: Orphan care is the call to lay down our lives for others just as Jesus laid down His life for us.

READ:
2 Corinthians 5:21 —

> *For our sake he made him to be sin who knew no sin, so that in him we might become the righteousness of God.*

2 Corinthians 8:9 —

> *For you know the grace of our Lord Jesus Christ, that though he was rich, yet for your sake he became poor, so that you by his poverty might become rich.*

The gospel is the story of a "great exchange" – God's righteousness for our unrighteousness, His holiness for our sin, the fullness of His glory for our emptiness. He suffered and died so that we could live.

. . . .

And like our Savior, who poured out His life and blood so we have reason to rejoice, we were made to lay down our lives and give until it hurts. We are most alive when we are loving and actively giving of ourselves because we were made to do these things. – Francis Chan

. . . .

Jesus laid down the infinite value of His own life so that we might know the immeasurable worth of being fully loved by Him. In a similar way, our call to care for the marginalized and orphaned is ultimately the call to accept the costs we may incur as worth it for the gain a child may receive through our love for them. This is nothing less than what Jesus has done for us, so we are compelled to do it for them. We must always keep this perspective, because when it gets hard and we begin to question whether or not the cost is worth it, it is being reminded of the gospel and the lengths Jesus went to call us His own that will carry us and sustain us through.

Orphan care will at times stretch the limits of who we are and what we are capable of. It will take us places emotionally, spiritually and even physically we never imagined. It will cost us, but in the end the value of the life of a child always far exceeds the value of anything we may have to lose in order to love that child.

Here's a short list of "costs" many can anticipate incurring in the call to care for orphans. *As a group, discuss some of these and see if you can think of any others:*

- ◆ Money
- ◆ Comfort
- ◆ The picture of the "ideal family"
- ◆ Your schedule
- ◆ Your car or house may be too small with an extra kid
- ◆ _____
- ◆ _____
- ◆ _____

Gospel-Centered vs. Family-Centered Thinking

Of all the gifts we can give an orphan, none is more precious than the safety and security of a loving family. The lack of this is what technically classifies a child as an orphan, so the provision of this in their lives brings about a monumental shift in their identity. Our care of orphans must be gospel-centered in scope, otherwise the tendency to be family-centered will dominate our motivations. To be gospel-centered means to always keep at the forefront of our thinking the belief that it is better to give than to receive, and that true service of others almost always involves true sacrifice of self.

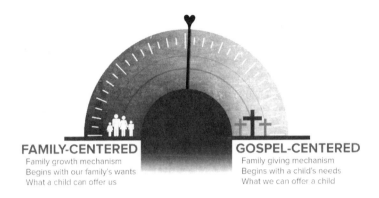

FAMILY-CENTERED
Family growth mechanism
Begins with our family's wants
What a child can offer us

GOSPEL-CENTERED
Family giving mechanism
Begins with a child's needs
What we can offer a child

If you were to take an honest evaluation of your heart today, where would you fall on this spectrum?

What steps can you take to increasingly move yourself towards a giving, gospel-centered posture?

Foster care and adoption are first family-giving mechanisms before they are family-growth mechanisms. They're not about getting a child for our family but rather giving our family for a child — and willingly embracing the implications that come along with that. That's not to say that a family can't grow through adoption — it obviously does — or that a family doesn't receive endless amounts of blessings and joy through foster care — it no doubt can. It is to say, however, that our first call is to give, not receive — to recognize that true service of others almost always involves true sacrifice of self. Only the gospel can produce that posture.

As a group, spend a few minutes discussing why it is important to distinguish between a family-centered approach and a gospel-centered one.

DISCUSS

As you close your time together, spend 5-10 minutes processing the things you have learned and discussed. This is an especially important opportunity to share thoughts, feelings, questions, concerns or any resolutions you have made in response to your study.

♦ What truth or idea stood out to you most in this session? Why?

♦ Why is it so important for us to understand the theology of the gospel as it pertains to our care of orphans?

♦ What concerns or fears do you have about the "costs" associated in caring for the marginalized, neglected, abused and orphaned? What specifically, if anything, comes to your mind immediately when we talk about the things you must be willing to "lose" in order for a child to gain?

REFLECT

As you reflect on the truths of this session and consider the personal implications for your own life, spend some time writing and processing through the following three concepts:

1. Write about some unique aspects of the gospel that stood out to you most in this session.

2. Write a letter to your family (maybe any current children you have, a spouse that is unsure about the calling to care for orphans, or any extended family that may be a part of helping support you as you care for children) explaining why you believe God is calling you to "give your family" (including them) to a child and what that could mean for everyone involved.

3. Write out a prayer to God, asking Him for the strength to always keep "giving" as your primary motivation and perspective. Ask Him for courage to take the next steps in the process to provide care for marginalized, abused and orphaned children and to willingly accept the costs as worth it for the gain a child may receive.

JOURNAL

—

_____

_____

_____

_____

_____

_____

_____

_____

_____

_____

_____

_____

_____

_____

_____

_____

THE OTHER SIDE OF ORPHAN CARE

—

God loves people enough to engage them where they are and loves them too much to allow them to stay there.

ALL IN ORPHAN CARE

 Before you begin, watch the Launch Video: Session 4 at www.allinorphancare.com/launch to help get you started.

PRAY
—

As you gather the group together, begin with prayer. Each group member should have the opportunity to share any particular requests they would like the group to pray for. Use this time as an opportunity to encourage one another and focus your hearts and minds on what God may have in store during your time together.

CONNECT
—

Spend the next 5-10 minutes connecting as a group. Catch up on what's going on in each other's lives.

- How has your week been?
- Did anything out of the ordinary or particularly interesting happen?
- Is anything coming up for you between now and the next group meeting that you want group members to know?

In Session 3, we looked at specific ways the gospel can vividly be displayed and tangibly demonstrated through the care of orphans. During this session, we will discuss the importance of proactively engaging families in their circumstances to prevent children from needing to be removed from their care.

As you begin this session, share your answers to the following questions with the group:

◆ Can you describe a time in your life when God protected you from something by preventing what was necessary to get you there from ever even happening?

◆ How did you feel at the time? What have you learned as a result of looking back on that time with a different perspective?

GROW

—

When God Prevents, God Protects

God intercedes on behalf of people. His character always bends Him towards the helpless and hurting, not away from them. His heart always compels Him to act for their good, never their harm. Consistently throughout Scripture, we see God stepping into people's circumstances, not simply to prevent them from engaging in certain behaviors but ultimately to protect them from the devastating consequences that those behaviors will bring about in their lives. His restrictions are always redemptive in purpose.

Let's look at a couple of examples of this in Scripture:

The Story of Jonah

Jonah was called by God to go to an evil city called Nineveh and preach repentance there. Instead, Jonah chose to go against the purpose of God and began traveling in the opposite direction towards a town called Tarshish. His journey would get a little precarious at times, and his attempts to run from God would ultimately end unsuccessfully.

Let's see why:

READ:
Jonah 1:4-16 —

The Lord hurled a great wind upon the sea, and there was a mighty tempest on the sea, so that the ship threatened to break up. Then the mariners were afraid, and each cried out to his god. And they hurled the cargo that was in the ship into the sea to lighten it for them. But Jonah had gone down into the inner part of the ship and had lain down and was fast asleep. So the captain came and said to him, "What do you mean, you sleeper? Arise, call out to your god! Perhaps the god will give a thought to us, that we may not perish."

They said to one another, "Come, let us cast lots, that we may know on whose account this evil has come upon us." So they cast lots, and the lot fell on Jonah. Then they said to him, "Tell us on whose account this evil has come upon us. What is your occupation? And where do you come from? What is your country? And of what people are you?" And he said to them, "I am a Hebrew, and I fear the Lord, the God of heaven, who made the sea and the dry land." Then the men were exceedingly afraid and said to him, "What is this that you have done!" For the men knew that he was fleeing from the presence of the Lord, because he had told them.

Then they said to him, "What shall we do to you, that the sea may quiet down for us?" For the sea grew more and more tempestuous. He said to them, "Pick me up and hurl me into the sea; then the sea will quiet down for you, for I know it is because of me that this great tempest has come upon you." Nevertheless, the men rowed hard1 to get back to dry land, but they could not, for the sea grew more and more tempestuous against them. Therefore they called out to the Lord, "O Lord, let us not perish for this man's life, and lay not on us innocent blood, for you, O Lord, have done as it pleased you." So they picked up Jonah and hurled him into the sea, and the sea ceased from its raging. Then the men feared the Lord exceedingly, and they offered a sacrifice to the Lord and made vows.

What about the sailors' reaction to the storm and Jonah's response to them stands out to you most in this passage?

Jonah is running from God. He's in self-destruct mode. When we read the story through this lens how should we view the storm? Is it Jonah's punishment or is it Jonah's rescue?

Explain how this storm, and Jonah subsequently being thrown overboard, can be viewed as God's merciful intervention in his life. What did it prevent him from doing? How did it protect him from the consequences of doing it?

READ:
Jonah 1:17 —

> *And the Lord appointed a great fish to swallow up Jonah. And Jonah was in the belly of the fish three days and three nights.*

Jonah 2:1, 10 —

> *Then Jonah prayed to the Lord his God from the belly of the fish ... and the Lord spoke to the fish, and it vomited Jonah out upon the dry land.*

God had already sent a storm to stop Jonah from arriving at Tarshish. How do we see Him continue to intervene in this passage?

We often think of the whale as punishment, and it, of course, is an uncomfortable place that Jonah found himself due to his disobedience. As uncomfortable as it may be, how can the belly of the whale be seen as the merciful intervention of God on behalf of Jonah?

Consider where Jonah was and what was about to happen to him before the whale swallowed him up. What did it prevent from occurring? How does this redefine or broaden our understanding of what God's mercy looks like, how it works and how it may sometimes feel in our lives?

The story of Jonah shows that God's heart is to mercifully intervene in the lives of those who are in self-destruct mode. His heart is to prevent us from the consequences of certain behaviors in order to protect us from the brokenness, loss, shame and despair those behaviors will ultimately lead to. His mercy is necessary no matter how uncomfortable it may be at the time.

The Story of the Woman at the Well

This unnamed woman, known most commonly as "the woman at the well," was a poor woman from Samaria who had quite a reputation. She had been married five times and was now living in sin with a man who wasn't her husband. On what seemed to be just another day of tasks of which included fetching water from a nearby well, she would meet Jesus and never be the same.

READ:
John 4:7-18 —

> A woman from Samaria came to draw water. Jesus said to her, "Give me a drink." (For his disciples had gone away into the city to buy food.) The Samaritan woman said to him, "How is it that you, a Jew, ask for a drink from me, a woman of Samaria?" (For Jews have no dealings with Samaritans.) Jesus answered her, "If you knew the gift of God, and who it is that is saying to you, 'Give me a drink,' you would have asked him, and he would have given you living water." The woman said to him, "Sir, you have nothing to draw water with, and the well is deep. Where do you get that living water? Are you greater than our father Jacob? He gave us the well and drank from it himself, as did his sons and his livestock." Jesus said to her, "Everyone who drinks of this water will be thirsty again, but whoever drinks of the water that I will give him will never be thirsty again. The water that I will give him will become in him a spring of water welling up to eternal life." The woman said to him, "Sir, give me this water, so that I will not be thirsty or have to come here to draw water."

> *Jesus said to her, "Go, call your husband, and come here."*
> *The woman answered him, "I have no husband." Jesus said*
> *to her, "You are right in saying, 'I have no husband'; for you*
> *have had five husbands, and the one you now have is not*
> *your husband. What you have said is true."*

This Samaritan woman is going about her daily business, all while hiding the dark secrets of her sordid and broken life. She asks Jesus for spiritual nourishment. What stands out to you about His response?

Jesus presses on the deepest parts of her shame, not to hurt her, but to heal her. How does His approach with her demonstrate love and mercy? How does it set her free from the consequences of continuing in her destructive behavior?

READ:
John 4:25-30 —

> *The woman said to him, "I know that Messiah is coming*
> *(he who is called Christ). When he comes, he will tell us all*
> *things." Jesus said to her, "I who speak to you am he."*
>
> *Just then his disciples came back. They marveled that he was*
> *talking with a woman, but no one said, "What do you seek?" or,*
> *"Why are you talking with her?" So the woman left her water jar*
> *and went away into town and said to the people, "Come, see*
> *a man who told me all that I ever did. Can this be the Christ?"*
> *They went out of the town and were coming to him.*

John 4:39-42 —

> *Many Samaritans from that town believed in him because of*
> *the woman's testimony, "He told me all that I ever did." So*
> *when the Samaritans came to him, they asked him to stay*
> *with them, and he stayed there two days. And many more*
> *believed because of his word. They said to the woman, "It is*
> *no longer because of what you said that we believe, for we*
> *have heard for ourselves, and we know that this is indeed*
> *the Savior of the world."*

What is her response to Jesus? Is she angry at Him for "meddling in her business"? Is she offended that He would step into her situation, expose it for what it was and then offer His hand as a solution?

What do we learn about God's intervention into people's lives who are in self-destruct mode through this story? What kind of impact did it have on her life and the lives of those around her?

The story of The Woman at the Well shows that Jesus came to save the sick, set the captive free and heal the hurting. He loves people enough to engage them where they are and loves them too much to allow them to stay there. He engages people in their darkest places in order to bring them into the light. He presses where it hurts at times, not to hurt but to heal, bring freedom and draw them into greater depths of intimacy with Himself.

The Two Sides Of Orphan Care

The goal in caring for orphans is always permanence – providing children the opportunity to grow up in a loving, supportive and nurturing family environment. This is the singular purpose for which all of our efforts are exclusively aimed. However, the means by which that one purpose are accomplished are two-fold:

1. Through restoration of and/or reunification with the family of origin.
2. Through adoption into a new forever family.

Both accomplish the goal of a child being raised in a permanent family structure – one involves a child from one family entering into another family, the other involves preventing a child from being permanently removed from their family through alternative forms of care.

One is reactive in nature, especially in foster care situations where a child may experience abuse or neglect and is in need of someone stepping in to protect them. Often times, the severity of circumstances requires swift and immediate measures to protect the rights of the vulnerable. This is a good and just solution to a very real problem and a pure reflection of the heart of God to intercede on behalf of the helpless and hopeless.

The other is proactive in nature, responding to the struggles of families and interceding with alternative forms of care — counseling, mentoring and rehabilitation efforts — to help keep families together. This too is right and honorable and a clear reflection of the heart of God to bring healing to what is broken and hope to what otherwise may have led to devastating consequences.

Both are necessary and both are essential.

Orphan care is bigger than just adopting children who have no families, it's also the responsibility we have, whenever possible, to do whatever is necessary to prevent kids from ever becoming orphans.

Consider this hypothetical, but very realistic story of a little boy we will call Johnny.

Johnny was born into a difficult environment. His father is in prison and his mother has struggled with drug addictions most of her adult life. She was using while pregnant with him, requiring state child welfare services to intervene after his birth in the hospital. Johnny was immediately removed from her care and placed in a local foster home. While this foster family was honored to care for Johnny, they were also devastated over the fact that it was brokenness and struggle that led him to them.

As the weeks and months of court hearings and parent visitations transpired, Johnny's foster parents learned more and more of his mother's story – she too had grown up in a home riddled with drug addiction and abuse. Those past generational patterns of brokenness evolved into her life and the effects were now perpetuating themselves into the life of her son. She was devastated over this and desperately needed help to get out from underneath the demons in her life that had been passed down to her and she was now passing down to him.

Johnny's foster parents began to understand that their involvement in his life was bigger than just him. They had stepped foot into the middle of generational cycles of brokenness and been given the opportunity to bring hope and healing – not just to a little boy, but to the family of that little boy as well.

In this hypothetical story of Johnny and his parents, we are reminded that the story of a struggling family and cycles of generational brokenness often precede our involvement in that child's life. Our care of vulnerable children is crucial, but so is our fuller awareness of the contexts from which they come.

Question: What is your current posture towards biological families? Fear? Anger? Uncertainty? Compassion?

Why is Prevention So Important?

It's impossible to get away from the fact that God loves us enough to mercifully intervene in our lives – to both prevent us from engaging in destructive behavior and protect us from the consequences of those behaviors. Not only does He love us enough to engage us where we are, as uncomfortable as it may be at times, He also loves us too much to allow us to stay there.

The reality of His proactive involvement in our lives in this capacity then begs the question of us:

How are we proactively, mercifully and lovingly interceding into the lives of broken and destitute families, as uncomfortable and hard as it may be at times, to bring hope and healing to an otherwise tragic situation?

This, too, is orphan care – working to prevent the need for more orphans to be cared for.

There are some pretty clear solutions that can be offered when it comes to responding to a child who is in need, whether it be offer a safe, temporary home for them, legally foster them or even provide permanence for them through adoption. However, the solutions are not so clearly defined when it comes to proactively engaging families in order to prevent children from being removed from their long-term care. At a minimum, our hope in this session is to expose both sides of orphan care and to bring awareness to the holistic picture of all that transpires in cases of child and family welfare. Perhaps, as you prayerfully discern where God is leading you to get involved, you will be drawn not only to the children but to the noble task of interceding on behalf of those children's families to bring about restoration long-term and prevent kids from needing to be removed.

DISCUSS

As you close your time together, spend 5-10 minutes processing the things you have learned and discussed. This is an especially important opportunity to share thoughts, feelings, questions, concerns or any resolutions you have made in response to your study.

◆ What truth or idea stood out to you most in this session? Why?

◆ Why is it important for us to understand both sides of the orphan care issue?

◆ What do the truths and ideas discussed in the session make you think about your own calling to care for the marginalized, abused and neglected?

REFLECT

As you reflect on the truths of this session and consider the personal implications for your own life, spend some time writing and processing through the following three questions:

1. What is your current posture and attitude towards the biological families of children who are in need of help? How can you ask God to increase your capacity to have compassion not just on the child, but on the family as well?

2. Having been exposed to "the other side of orphan care," what questions, fears or concerns do you have

about what that might mean for you as you seek to live out the heart of God by interceding on behalf of the marginalized and oppressed?

3. Consider again the "parameters" you have defined for how you want to engage in orphan care. Are you willing to let God expand those and have you step into areas of involvement you were not necessarily preparing yourself for? Why? Why not?

JOURNAL

—

_____

_____

_____

_____

_____

_____

_____

_____

_____

_____

_____

_____

_____

_____

_____

_____

SAYING YES TO THE MESSY

—

Jocelyn Hattenberger

Foster Mom to 13

Adoptive Mom to 3

I can remember driving to that first family visitation. Even after 2 years of being a foster parent, facing the biological mother for the first time was anxiety inducing, never knowing what I would be walking into.

I listened to the 2-month-old screaming in the back seat as I drove and anger welled up inside me as it did day after day thinking about what his tiny body was going through. Born positive for 10 different drugs in his system, and finally weaned off of morphine and methadone, he was an addict coming off of drugs. Everything was over-stimulating to him, he couldn't control his own body temperature, he had tremors in his arms and legs and a cry that I was sure could crack glass.

And here we were on our way to meet the woman who birthed an addict. And I was angry. How dare she? What is wrong with this woman? How could she be so selfish? Does she have any idea what she has done to her precious child? The questions and judgments swirled in my head.

I entered the building ready to see the shameless drug addict I had judged as worthless and depraved. Instead, I met a teenager whose eyes could not meet mine as she meekly asked if she could hold her baby. As we sat waiting for the caseworker, she began to talk, pouring out her soul and telling me her story of years of dysfunction and abuse I could not even fathom living through. As I listened, my heart ached and my judgments of her became regrettable, distant thoughts in need of repentance.

At the next visitation, she brought me a rose and asked me a question that has never left my heart. "Can you teach me how to feed him and what to do if he is crying, and things that a mom should be able to do?" Three months later, I placed him in her arms at a rehabilitation facility where he would live with her with a stack of reminder notes of "things that a mom should be able to do." She held on to our hug so tightly as she cried tears of happiness, and it clicked in my heart that foster care could be (and more importantly, as a Christian, should be) more than about taking a child into my home.

Fostering means saying "yes" to the messy and being pulled into worlds you never knew actually existed, just miles away from your comfortable, well-decorated, clean, safe home. Being a foster parent means not only fostering love and hope into the life of a child, but also into the life of the biological family that comes with that child.

This is not an easy thing to do and doesn't always come naturally. When I am holding a hurting baby and learning about the abuse and neglect they have suffered, or confronted with an angry and irrational parent, my first reaction is not to show grace and love. But I am reminded how once, while I was still in the midst of my own dysfunction and sin, I was shown grace and love by a Savior who had nothing to gain in extending His mercy. There is no greater way to show the love and grace of our Father than to extend that grace to a hurting world — and that includes biological parents of a child in my home.

On one of the most exciting days in the life of a foster parent — the arrival of a child to care for — there is another parent, another family experiencing one of the worst days of their lives — the removal of their child from their home. If I can do nothing else but offer them a smile, a kind word, understanding in the midst of anger and fear then I have shown a grace I was once shown myself. As I am caring for and loving a child I have been blessed to foster, may I never forget there is a hurting parent on the other side who is in great need of kindness and grace possibly for the first time in their lives.

MAKING ORPHAN CARE "SMALL"

—

*You may not be able to change the world for everyone,
but you can change the world of someone.*

Before you begin, watch the Launch Video: Session 5 at www.allinorphancare.com/launch to help get you started.

PRAY

—

As you gather the group together, begin with prayer. Each group member should have the opportunity to share any particular requests they would like the group to pray for. Use this time as an opportunity to encourage one another and focus your hearts and minds on what God may have in store during your time together.

CONNECT

—

Spend the next 5-10 minutes connecting as a group. Catch up on what's going on in each other's lives.

- How has your week been?
- Did anything out of the ordinary or particularly interesting happen?
- Is anything coming up for you between now and the next group meeting that you want group members to know?

In Session 4, we looked at "the other side of orphan care" and were exposed to the reality of the contexts many marginalized, abused and neglected children come from. In this session, we will spend time looking at some current statistics that will help give us a picture of what the global and domestic orphan care crisis looks like. We'll see that the need is overwhelming, but our opportunity to make a difference is very real. Jesus is changing the world one person at a time, and so can we.

As you begin this session, share your answers to the following questions with the group:

- Can you describe a time in your life when someone went out of their way to serve you, make you feel special or love you in ways that you very specifically needed at the time?

- How did that make you feel? Looking back on it now, how has it helped shape the person that you are today?

GROW
—

Changing the World of One

The Kingdom of God redefines and reorients most of what the world says is valuable and worth giving our lives over to. Jesus is constantly inverting the order of things and setting into a motion a new and better way of living. He says the first will be last and the last will be first (Matthew 20:16), if you want to find your life you must first lose it (Luke 9:24) and the least likely among you usually ends up being the greatest (Luke 9:48). His message consistently represented a reversal of the world's values.

This theme carries through into some very familiar parables Jesus uses to illustrate the lengths to which He would go in order to save just one soul.

READ:
Luke 15:1-32 —

> Now the tax collectors and sinners were all drawing near to hear him. And the Pharisees and the scribes grumbled, saying, "This man receives sinners and eats with them."
>
> So he told them this parable: "What man of you, having a

hundred sheep, if he has lost one of them, does not leave
the ninety-nine in the open country, and go after the one that
is lost, until he finds it? And when he has found it, he lays it
on his shoulders, rejoicing. And when he comes home, he
calls together his friends and his neighbors, saying to them,
'Rejoice with me, for I have found my sheep that was lost.'
Just so, I tell you, there will be more joy in heaven over one
sinner who repents than over ninety-nine righteous persons
who need no repentance.

"Or what woman, having ten silver coins, if she loses one
coin, does not light a lamp and sweep the house and seek
diligently until she finds it? And when she has found it, she
calls together her friends and neighbors, saying, 'Rejoice
with me, for I have found the coin that I had lost.' Just so,
I tell you, there is joy before the angels of God over one
sinner who repents."

And he said, "There was a man who had two sons. And the
younger of them said to his father, 'Father, give me the share
of property that is coming to me.' And he divided his property
between them. Not many days later, the younger son gathered
all he had and took a journey into a far country, and there he
squandered his property in reckless living. And when he had
spent everything, a severe famine arose in that country, and
he began to be in need. So he went and hired himself out to
one of the citizens of that country, who sent him into his fields
to feed pigs. And he was longing to be fed with the pods that
the pigs ate, and no one gave him anything.

"But when he came to himself, he said, 'How many of my
father's hired servants have more than enough bread, but
I perish here with hunger! I will arise and go to my father,
and I will say to him, "Father, I have sinned against heaven
and before you. I am no longer worthy to be called your son.
Treat me as one of your hired servants."' And he arose and
came to his father. But while he was still a long way off, his
father saw him and felt compassion, and ran and embraced

him and kissed him. And the son said to him, 'Father, I have sinned against heaven and before you. I am no longer worthy to be called your son.' But the father said to his servants, 'Bring quickly the best robe, and put it on him, and put a ring on his hand, and shoes on his feet. And bring the fattened calf and kill it, and let us eat and celebrate. For this my son was dead, and is alive again; he was lost, and is found.' And they began to celebrate.

"Now his older son was in the field, and as he came and drew near to the house, he heard music and dancing. And he called one of the servants and asked what these things meant. And he said to him, 'Your brother has come, and your father has killed the fattened calf, because he has received him back safe and sound.' But he was angry and refused to go in. His father came out and entreated him, but he answered his father, 'Look, these many years I have served you, and I never disobeyed your command, yet you never gave me a young goat, that I might celebrate with my friends. But when this son of yours came, who has devoured your property with prostitutes, you killed the fattened calf for him!' And he said to him, 'Son, you are always with me, and all that is mine is yours. It was fitting to celebrate and be glad, for this your brother was dead, and is alive; he was lost, and is found.'"

- ◆ How do these illustrations represent a reversal of the world's value system?
- ◆ What do we learn about the lengths God would go to in order to save just one?

While the world may say the 99 sheep are clearly more valuable, Jesus was deeply concerned about the one; while the nine coins seem to be enough, Jesus was still very much focused on the one; while a brother still remained at home, Jesus sought out the one who needed to be brought back.

Jesus always carried a great burden for the masses but never neglected the importance of each individual He encountered. He set out to change the world and in many ways did so one person at a time.

READ:

Luke 19:1-5 —

> He entered Jericho and was passing through. And behold, there was a man named Zacchaeus. He was a chief tax collector and was rich. And he was seeking to see who Jesus was, but on account of the crowd he could not, because he was small in stature. So he ran on ahead and climbed up into a sycamore tree to see him, for he was about to pass that way. And when Jesus came to the place, he looked up and said to him, "Zacchaeus, hurry and come down, for I must stay at your house today."

Mark 5:21-34 —

> And when Jesus had crossed again in the boat to the other side, a great crowd gathered about him, and he was beside the sea. Then came one of the rulers of the synagogue, Jairus by name, and seeing him, he fell at his feet and implored him earnestly, saying, "My little daughter is at the point of death. Come and lay your hands on her, so that she may be made well and live." And he went with him.
>
> And a great crowd followed him and thronged about him. And there was a woman who had had a discharge of blood for twelve years, and who had suffered much under many physicians, and had spent all that she had, and was no better but rather grew worse. She had heard the reports about Jesus and came up behind him in the crowd and touched his garment. For she said, "If I touch even his garments, I will be made well." And immediately the flow of blood dried up, and she felt in her body that she was healed of her disease. And Jesus, perceiving in himself that power had gone out from him, immediately turned about in the crowd and said, "Who touched my garments?" And his disciples said to him, "You see the crowd pressing around

you, and yet you say, 'Who touched me?'" And he looked around to see who had done it. But the woman, knowing what had happened to her, came in fear and trembling and fell down before him and told him the whole truth. And he said to her, "Daughter, your faith has made you well; go in peace, and be healed of your disease."

- How do these stories reflect Jesus' concern for the individual even when the masses are crowding around Him?

- What stands out to you most in these stories? What do you appreciate most about Jesus' response?

Making Orphan Care "Small"

While fostering, adopting and caring for abused, neglected, marginalized and orphaned children is a big deal, we must learn to *scale it down* and make it "small," otherwise we might get lost in its massiveness.

. . . .

"Do your little bit of good where you are; it's those little bits of good put together that overwhelm the world." – Desmond Tutu

. . . .

The call to care for orphans doesn't mean you have to change the world for them ALL; it does mean, however, you can change the world of at least ONE. God doesn't expect us to do everything for everyone; He does expect us to do something for someone.

Start with coming alongside one, loving one, caring for one and making sure that at least one knows they are valued and treasured. Start with one. Remember, behind the numbers and the stats are real kids facing real issues in need of real help.

Understanding the Need

Here are some recent statistics[1] that help us understand the current orphan care landscape worldwide and right here at home:

- According to UNICEF estimates[2], there are 17,900,000 orphans who have lost both parents and are living in orphanages or on the streets and lack the care and attention required for healthy development.

- In the U.S., 400,540 children are living without permanent families in the foster care system. 115,000 of these children are eligible for adoption, but nearly 40% of these children will wait over three years in foster care before being adopted.

- Each year, over 27,000 youth "age out" of foster care without the emotional and financial support necessary to succeed.

- As of 2011, nearly 60,000 children in foster care in the U.S. are placed in institutions or group homes, not in traditional foster homes.

- The average length of time a child waits to be adopted in foster care is over three years. Roughly 55% of these children have had three or more placements. One study found that 33% of children had changed elementary schools five or more times, losing relationships and falling behind educationally.

The statistics are daunting: millions of orphans around the world - hundreds of thousands within the United States, dozens of thousands within your state and city, hundreds and thousands within your community alone - needing a caring family, a safe place to call home, parents to love them and someone to tell them they matter and that everything is going to be ok. This is the reality of the world

1   Source: http://www.unicef.org/sowc2013/files/SWCR2013_ENG_Lo_res_24_Apr_2013.pdf

2   Source: http://thegospelcoalition.org/blogs/tgc/2013/11/07/9-things-you-should-know-about-orphans/

in which we live, but with numbers like that it's hard to wrap our minds around what to do, where to go and how to even begin to be a solution to the problem.

Every number represents a child — a real child with a real story in need of real help. We must always keep our perspective in this place. We may never change the whole world for every child, but we can at least change the world of one child.

DISCUSS
As you close your time together, spend 5-10 minutes processing the things you have learned and discussed. This is an especially important opportunity to share thoughts, feelings, questions, concerns or any resolutions you have made in response to your study.

- What truth or idea stood out to you most in this session? Why?

- Why is it important for us to not get so overwhelmed with the great need out there?

- What do the truths and ideas discussed in the session make you think about your own calling to care for the marginalized, abused and neglected?

REFLECT
As you reflect on the truths of this session and consider the personal implications for your own life, spend some time writing and processing through the following three questions:

1. How does making orphan care "small" help you think through what role you can play in caring for marginalized, abused and orphaned children?

2. What impact do you hope to make on the life of at least one child? What things do you want them to be able to say about your involvement in their life as they grow up?

3. Consider the legacy you can leave and the generational impact you can make on the life of one child. What thoughts, dreams, fears and joys come to mind? What excites you the most about the possibilities?

JOURNAL
—

—

IDENTIFYING YOUR ROLE

—

No one is called to do everything, but everyone is called to do something.

*Before you begin, watch the Launch Video: Session 6
at www.allinorphancare.com/launch to help get you started.*

PRAY

—

As you gather the group together, begin with prayer. Each group member should have the opportunity to share any particular requests they would like the group to pray for. Use this time as an opportunity to encourage one another and focus your hearts and minds on what God may have in store during your time together.

CONNECT

—

Spend the next 5-10 minutes connecting as a group. Catch up on what's going on in each other's lives.

- How has your week been?
- Did anything out of the ordinary or particularly interesting happen?
- Is anything coming up for you between now and the next group meeting that you want group members to know?

In Session 5, we talked about making orphan care "small" and doing your part to make a difference in the life of at least one child. During this session, we will take a biblical look at how the Body of Christ is called to operate together — each member serving different functions but all functions being of equal importance. Specifically, we will look at how the Body of Christ can serve the cause of the marginalized, abused and orphaned in different but equally important ways.

The Bible says every believer has been given a unique set of spiritual gifts. Have you ever identified yours?

Spiritual Gifts Survey

Before you begin this study, spend the next 10-15 minutes silently and quickly answering the questions in the Spiritual Gifts Survey on page 111, determining your "scores" and sharing your top 3 results with the group.

GROW
—

One Body, Many Parts

The imagery of a human body is consistently used throughout Scripture to illustrate the identity and activity of the Church — how the people of God relate with each other and work together. Ultimately, unique gifts are given to unique individuals, not for their own good but for the good of the whole body. Within the Body of Christ roles are established not on the basis of rank, as if one person's position was more important than another, but on the premise that when each member fulfills their responsibility the whole body will function better for it.

READ:
1 Corinthians 12:4-7 —

> *Now there are varieties of gifts, but the same Spirit; and there are varieties of service, but the same Lord; and there are varieties of activities, but it is the same God who empowers them all in everyone. To each is given the manifestation of the Spirit for the common good.*

◆ What stands out to you most in this passage?

◆ What do we learn about uniqueness, diversity and unity in the Body of Christ? Based on these verses, how would you define "unity"?

READ:
1 Corinthians 12:18-19, 27 —

> *But as it is, God arranged the members in the body, each one of them, as he chose. If all were a single member, where would the body be?...Now you are the body of Christ and individually members of it.*

- ♦ How are we to understand the role we have been given in the Body? Has God made any mistakes in giving some people certain gifts and callings and other people different ones?

- ♦ What does this passage communicate about the essential nature of our diverse roles?

- ♦ Discuss the tone of this passage. Does it seem to suggest your role in the Body is optional?

The proper functioning of the people of God to fulfill the purposes of God are always portrayed in communal terms, not individualistic ones. Everyone has a role to play, but not everyone is called to play the same role. The call to care for the marginalized, oppressed, abused, neglected and orphaned in this world is for all — we all have a role to play, there are no exceptions. The question is not "Am I supposed to get involved?" but rather, "HOW am I supposed to get involved?"

. . . .

"Each of us has a role to play, and every role is important. There is no small service to God; it all matters." — Rick Warren

. . . .

Opportunities to Get Involved

While the call is to all, the opportunities to respond are limitless and full of possibilities. No one can do everything, but everyone can do something. You may not be called to bring a child into your home, but you can certainly play a role in serving and supporting those who do. Or perhaps you will bring children into your home on short-term arrangements while others will foster and/or adopt more long-term. Again, no one can do everything, but everyone can do something. Here are some common, practical ways to care for vulnerable children and their families or to simply provide care and support for those who are.

Foster Care

Foster care is a temporary living arrangement for abused, neglected, and dependent children who need a safe place (homes or treatment centers) to live when their parents or another relative cannot take care of them. Foster families are recruited, trained, and licensed to care for abused and neglected children temporarily, while their parents work with social work professionals to resolve their family issues. In cases where the child becomes free for adoption, foster parents may be considered as adoptive parents.

Adoption

Adoption is a legal process that permanently gives parental rights to adoptive parents. Adoption means taking a child into your home as a permanent family member. There are opportunities to adopt through the foster care system, private domestic agencies and international agencies. Adoption finalizes a child's permanent placement into his/her new family.

Respite Care

Respite care is basically short-term foster care. It is primarily used to provide aid to other foster families needing childcare for more than 24 hours and less than 14 days. This is extremely helpful as situations often come up in which the family must travel and can't take the child due to state rules. Respite care gives foster, adoptive, and kinship parents and children the chance to have short, regular periods of time apart in which they can rest and recharge. It also provides crisis care for the times in which the trauma of the child is seriously impacting other members of the family.

Babysitting

In the world of orphan care, getting a babysitter isn't the easiest thing. In fact, it's somewhat of a process. You can support foster families by becoming a certified babysitter. This allows you to provide child care for foster families so parents can have an occasional time to "get away." This is an invaluable gift to a foster family and is always much appreciated. Generally, a background check and CPR/First Aid certification are required.

CASA

Court Appointed Special Advocates (CASA) volunteers are appointed by judges to watch over and advocate for abused and neglected children, to make sure they don't get overlooked by the legal and social system. In many ways, CASA advocates help speak for the child. They are of tremendous value in seeing that the child's best interests are protected.

Safe Families

Safe Families for Children™ provides a temporary safe environment for children while giving the parents a chance to get back on their feet before abuse or neglect occur. Parents experiencing a temporary crisis can arrange for their children to stay with families of faith so they can manage the issues that led to their crisis situation.

Financial Supporter

Whether you're able to write a $500 check or organize fundraisers online for cash, donating to a family who wants to adopt is a much needed and very fulfilling way to answer the call to orphan care.

General Resourcing

Many foster care and adoption placements happen with little to no advance notice. This usually means that needs can come up quickly. Donations of gift cards, diapers, and new supplies such as strollers, mattresses, car seats, and other necessities are invaluable for those who are bringing children into their homes.

Think "Outside the Box"

Get creative! Mow foster families yards for them. Host a parents' night out for foster and adoptive couples at church. Organize back-to-school drives to collect supplies for local foster children. Throw a big Christmas party for foster families and children. The opportunities to serve, support and show appreciation are endless. Get creative!

DISCUSS

As you close your time together, spend 5-10 minutes processing the things you have learned and discussed. This is an especially important opportunity to share thoughts, feelings, questions, concerns or any resolutions you have made in response to your study.

- ◆ What truth or idea stood out to you most in this session? Why?

- ◆ Why is it important for us to understand the unique passions, interests and gifts God has given us? How does our ability (and inability) to recognize these things help (or hurt) the Body of Christ as a whole?

- ◆ How is God calling you to get involved? Share with the group your thought processes, fears, questions and excitements about how you feel God may be leading you.

REFLECT

As you reflect on the truths of this session and consider the personal implications for your own life, spend some time writing and processing through the following three questions:

1. How has God uniquely wired you? What unique passions and interests has He given you that He wants you to use for the care of orphans?

2. What, if anything, is holding you back from using those

gifts and passions? Why? How?

3. What are your "next steps"? Making the next phone call, filling out the next form, attending the next class, sending the next email? Put down into words what your next step is, and share it with those around you who can hold you accountable to taking it. You have a role to play... what is it?

JOURNAL

—

_____

_____

_____

_____

_____

_____

_____

_____

_____

_____

_____

_____

_____

_____

_____

_____

ADDITIONAL RESOURCES

SPIRITUAL GIFTS SURVEY

—

DIRECTIONS

This is not a test, so there are no wrong answers. The **_Spiritual Gifts Survey_** consists of 80 statements. Some items reflect concrete actions; other items are descriptive traits; and still others are statements of belief.

- Select the one response you feel best characterizes yourself and place that number in the blank provided. Record your answer in the blank beside each item.

- Do not spend too much time on any one item. Remember, it is not a test. Usually your immediate response is best.

- Please give an answer for each item. Do not skip any items.

- Do not ask others how they are answering or how they think you should answer.

- Work at your own pace.

Your response choices are:

5—Highly characteristic of me/definitely true for me

4—Most of the time this would describe me/be true for me

3—Frequently characteristic of me/true for me-about 50 percent of the time

2—Occasionally characteristic of me/true for me-about 25 percent of the time

1—Not at all characteristic of me/definitely untrue for me

_____ 1. I have the ability to organize ideas, resources, time, and people effectively.

_____ 2. I am willing to study and prepare for the task of teaching.

_____ 3. I am able to relate the truths of God to specific situations.

_____ 4. I have a God-given ability to help others grow in their faith.

_____ 5. I possess a special ability to communicate the truth of salvation.

_____ 6. I have the ability to make critical decisions when necessary.

_____ 7. I am sensitive to the hurts of people.

_____ 8. I experience joy in meeting needs through sharing possessions.

_____ 9. I enjoy studying.

_____ 10. I have delivered God's message of warning and judgment.

_____ 11. I am able to sense the true motivation of persons and movements.

_____ 12. I have a special ability to trust God in difficult situations.

_____ 13. I have a strong desire to contribute to the establishment of new churches.

_____ 14. I take action to meet physical and practical needs rather than merely talking about or planning to help.

_____ 15. I enjoy entertaining guests in my home.

_____ 16. I can adapt my guidance to fit the maturity of those working with me.

_____ 17. I can delegate and assign meaningful work.

_____ 18. I have an ability and desire to teach.

_____ 19. I am usually able to analyze a situation correctly.

_____ 20. I have a natural tendency to encourage others.

_____ 21. I am willing to take the initiative in helping other Christians grow in their faith.

_____ 22. I have an acute awareness of the emotions of other people, such as loneliness, pain, fear, and anger.

_____ 23. I am a cheerful giver.

_____ 24. I spend time digging into facts.

_____ 25. I feel that I have a message from God to deliver to others.

_____ 26. I can recognize when a person is genuine/honest.

_____ 27. I am a person of vision (a clear mental portrait of a preferable future given by God). I am able to communicate vision in such a way that others commit to making the vision a reality.

_____ 28. I am willing to yield to God's will rather than question and waver.

_____ 29. I would like to be more active in getting the gospel to people in other lands.

_____ 30. It makes me happy to do things for people in need.

_____ 31. I am successful in getting a group to do its work joyfully.

_____ 32. I am able to make strangers feel at ease.

_____ 33. I have the ability to plan learning approaches.

_____ 34. I can identify those who need encouragement.

_____ 35. I have trained Christians to be more obedient disciples of Christ.

_____ 36. I am willing to do whatever it takes to see others come to Christ.

_____ 37. I am attracted to people who are hurting.

_____ 38. I am a generous giver.

_____ 39. I am able to discover new truths.

_____ 40. I have spiritual insights from Scripture concerning issues and people that compel me to speak out.

_____ 41. I can sense when a person is acting in accord with God's will.

_____ 42. I can trust in God even when things look dark.

_____ 43. I can determine where God wants a group to go and help it get there.

_____ 44. I have a strong desire to take the gospel to places where it has never been heard.

_____ 45. I enjoy reaching out to new people in my church and community.

_____ 46. I am sensitive to the needs of people.

_____ 47. I have been able to make effective and efficient plans for accomplishing the goals of a group.

_____ 48. I often am consulted when fellow Christians are struggling to make difficult decisions.

_____ 49. I think about how I can comfort and encourage others in my congregation.

_____ 50. I am able to give spiritual direction to others.

_____ 51. I am able to present the gospel to lost persons in such a way that they accept the Lord and His salvation.

_____ 52. I possess an unusual capacity to understand the feelings of those in distress.

_____ 53. I have a strong sense of stewardship based on the recognition that God owns all things.

_____ 54. I have delivered to other persons messages that have come directly from God.

_____ 55. I can sense when a person is acting under God's leadership.

_____ 56. I try to be in God's will continually and be available for His use.

_____ 57. I feel that I should take the gospel to people who have different beliefs from me.

_____ 58. I have an acute awareness of the physical needs of others.

_____ 59. I am skilled in setting forth positive and precise steps of action.

_____ 60. I like to meet visitors at church and make them feel welcome.

_____ 61. I explain Scripture in such a way that others understand it.

_____ 62. I can usually see spiritual solutions to problems.

_____ 63. I welcome opportunities to help people who need comfort, consolation, encouragement, and counseling.

_____ 64. I feel at ease in sharing Christ with nonbelievers.

_____ 65. I can influence others to perform to their highest God-given potential.

_____ 66. I recognize the signs of stress and distress in others.

_____ 67. I desire to give generously and unpretentiously to worthwhile projects and ministries.

_____ 68. I can organize facts into meaningful relationships.

_____ 69. God gives me messages to deliver to His people.

_____ 70. I am able to sense whether people are being honest when they tell of their religious experiences.

_____ 71. I enjoy presenting the gospel to persons of other cultures and backgrounds.

_____ 72. I enjoy doing little things that help people.

_____ 73. I can give a clear, uncomplicated presentation.

_____ 74. I have been able to apply biblical truth to the specific needs of my church.

_____ 75. God has used me to encourage others to live Christlike lives.

_____ 76. I have sensed the need to help other people become more effective in their ministries.

_____ 77. I like to talk about Jesus to those who do not know Him.

_____ 78. I have the ability to make strangers feel comfortable in my home.

_____ 79. I have a wide range of study resources and know how to secure information.

_____ 80. I feel assured that a situation will change for the glory of God even when the situation seem impossible.

SCORING YOUR SURVEY

Follow these directions to figure your score for each spiritual gift.

1. Place in each box your numerical response (1-5) to the item number which is indicated below the box.

2. For each gift, add the numbers in the boxes and put the total in the TOTAL box.

LEADERSHIP	+	+	+	+	=
	Item 6	Item 16	Item 27	Item 43	Item 65	TOTAL

ADMINISTRATION	+	+	+	+	=
	Item 1	Item 17	Item 31	Item 47	Item 59	TOTAL

TEACHING	+	+	+	+	=
	Item 2	Item 18	Item 33	Item 61	Item 73	TOTAL

KNOWLEDGE	+	+	+	+	=
	Item 9	Item 24	Item 39	Item 68	Item 79	TOTAL

WISDOM	+	+	+	+	=
	Item 3	Item 19	Item 48	Item 62	Item 74	TOTAL

PROPHECY	+	+	+	+	=
	Item 10	Item 25	Item 40	Item 54	Item 69	TOTAL

DISCERNMENT	+	+	+	+	=
	Item 11	Item 26	Item 41	Item 55	Item 70	TOTAL

EXHORTATION	+	+	+	+	=
	Item 20	Item 34	Item 49	Item 63	Item 75	TOTAL

SHEPHERDING	+	+	+	+	=
	Item 4	Item 21	Item 35	Item 50	Item 76	TOTAL

FAITH	+	+	+	+	=
	Item 12	Item 28	Item 42	Item 56	Item 80	TOTAL

EVANGELISM	+	+	+	+	=
	Item 5	Item 36	Item 51	Item 64	Item 77	TOTAL

APOSTLESHIP	+	+	+	+	=
	Item 13	Item 29	Item 44	Item 57	Item 71	TOTAL

SERVICE/HELPS	+	+	+	+	=	
	Item 14	Item 30	Item 46	Item 58	Item 72	TOTAL
MERCY	+	+	+	+	=	
	Item 7	Item 22	Item 37	Item 52	Item 66	TOTAL
GIVING	+	+	+	+	=	
	Item 8	Item 23	Item 38	Item 53	Item 67	TOTAL
HOSPITALITY	+	+	+	+	=	
	Item 15	Item 32	Item 45	Item 60	Item 78	TOTAL

____ Leadership ____ Shepherding

____ Administration ____ Faith

____ Teaching ____ Evangelism

____ Knowledge ____ Apostleship

____ Wisdom ____ Service/Helps

____ Prophecy ____ Mercy

____ Discernment ____ Giving

____ Exhortation ____ Hospitality

Now that you have completed the survey, thoughtfully answer the following questions.

The gifts I have begun to discover in my life are:

1. _____

2. _____

3. _____

For a detailed description of each of the spiritual gifts, visit
allinorphancare.com

ABOUT ARROW

—

ARROW CHILD & FAMILY MINISTRIES
Helping Kids - Strengthening Families

Serving children and families of the greater Houston community for the past 23 years, Arrow Child & Family Ministries is a Christian provider of child welfare and education services for abused and neglected children and families in crisis. Through the engagement of both government and the local church, Arrow provides an array of services including foster care, adoption, child sex trafficking recovery, and specialized education. All programs and services advance the well-being of children, families and communities while promoting Christian responsibility and a commitment to strengthen family life.

Foster Care

Arrow recruits and trains foster parents to open their homes to children rescued from abuse or neglect, as well as provide essential therapeutic services.

Adoption

Arrow facilitates private adoptions and the adoption of children in the foster care system whose birth parents have had their rights terminated by the courts.

Child Sex Trafficking Recovery

Freedom Place is a comprehensive, Christ-centered, long term care and recovery center serving underage female victims of domestic child sex trafficking.

Specialized Education

Arrow operates private, special education day schools that help emotionally disturbed adolescents reach their potential academically, emotionally and behaviorally.

Arrow International

Casa de Ester provides academic, spiritual and life skills training programs for up to 30 teenage girls in Tegucigalpa, Honduras who have been victims of sexual abuse.

ARROW FOUNDATION

The ALL IN Orphan Care material is a ministry resource created by Arrow Foundation, an affiliate organization founded by Arrow Child & Family Ministries in 2013. The mission of Arrow Foundation is to engage and equip the Church to care for the marginalized, neglected, abused and orphaned through foster care, adoption, family support services and other alternative forms of care.

The primary church engagement mechanism of Arrow Foundation is ALL IN, a collection of resources designed to teach, train, equip and mobilize the Church to help kids and strengthen families.

Through fundraising efforts, community collaboration initiatives and the development of church equipping resources, Arrow Foundation works to change the culture of child welfare across the country and throughout the world.

MARK TENNANT, FOUNDER

 Mark Tennant's unique journey of helping kids and strengthening families began as an 11-year-old child when he was removed from an abusive home and became a foster child himself. Eventually, Mark was placed in the Christian foster home of Bill and Joan Mack. It was the Mack's spiritual influence and their commitment to love Mark unconditionally that sparked Mark's own faith.

Coming to understand there was a calling on his life, Mark earned a

Pastoral Degree from Oral Roberts University. After graduation, he worked for several years in both church and child and family service administration until his calling became clear. In 1992, Mark founded Arrow Child & Family Ministries to help other abused and neglected children find foster families like his, so their lives could also be transformed.

Headquartered in Houston, Texas, with offices in Maryland, Pennsylvania and California, Arrow serves nearly 4,000 children and families each year through foster care, adoption and a wide range of social services and specialized education. Arrow also established "Freedom Place" in Texas, a rehabilitative center for victims of child sex trafficking, and "Casa de Ester," a girls' home in Honduras.

The heart of Arrow is rooted in Psalm 127:3-4, which Mark quotes frequently as the inspiration behind the work they do: "Children are a gift from the Lord...like arrows in the hand of a warrior so are the children of one's youth."

Mark lives in the Houston, TX area with his wife Kristy and three children.

To learn more about the work of Arrow, visit **www.arrow.org**.

ABOUT THE AUTHOR

—

 Jason Johnson grew up in the Dallas, TX area in a ministry oriented home. While attending Texas A&M University, Jason began working in ministry himself while on staff at a church. After earning his Speech Communications degree, Jason continued working in full-time pastoral ministry while studying at Dallas Theological Seminary.

With over 13 years of ministry experience, six of which include planting and leading a church within the Acts 29 Network, Jason has a deep passion to see the people of God equipped and mobilized to live out the mandate of God in this world.

As a frequent writer and speaker on issues of foster care, adoption and child welfare, Jason's passion comes from his own childhood story, his heart for the Church and from his personal experience as a licensed foster and adoptive parent.

Jason serves as the Church Engagement Officer with Arrow Foundation, is the primary content creator for ALL IN and blogs regularly at jasonjohnsonblog.com. He and his wife, Emily, met on campus at Texas A&M and were married a few weeks after graduation in 2002.

They currently live in the Houston, TX area with their four daughters, the youngest adopted through the foster care system in December 2013.